Solent Steam

Kevin McCormack

Ian Allan PUBLISHING

Front cover: With the Isle of Wight ferry to Yarmouth moored in the harbour, Standard Class 4 tank No 80032 leaves Lymington Pier for Brockenhurst in September 1966. Steam was replaced by diesel between April 1967 and the implementation in July 1967 of electrification, preparations for which are evident by the insulator pots beside the track. *Nick Lera*

Back cover: On 4 May 1958 appropriately named Class O2 No 17 *Seaview* stands half a mile out to sea at Ryde Pier Head station. The original station was Ryde St John's Road, but to make their ferry services more attractive the London & South Western Railway (LSWR) and the London, Brighton & South Coast Railway (LBSCR) built this seaward extension, owned jointly by the two companies. *Neil Davenport*

Previous page: Unrebuilt 'West Country' Pacific No 34099 *Lynmouth* heads the 'Bournemouth Belle' between Bournemouth West and Bournemouth Central on 22 April 1962. This prestigious train was withdrawn at the end of Southern steam on 9 July 1967 and during its final months was rostered for diesel haulage, although steam was sometimes substituted. *Jim Oatway*

Left: Still in London, Midland & Scottish Railway (LMS) livery and displaying its former number, Class 2P 4-4-0 No 698 (by now officially 40698) enters Bournemouth West station on 1 April 1949 with an S&D train. At the time, this line linking Bath and Bournemouth was operated jointly by the London Midland and Southern Regions. *Neil Davenport*

First published 2010

ISBN 978 0 7110 3426 6

All rights reserved. No part of this book ma by any means, electronic or mechanical, in by any information storage and retrieval sy permission from the Publisher in writing.

© Ian Allan Publishing Ltd 2010

Published by Ian Allan Publishing

an imprint of Ian Allan Publishing Ltd, Hersham, Surrey KT12 4RG.
Printed in England by Ian Allan Printing Ltd, Hersham, Surrey KT12 4RG.

Visit the Ian Allan Publishing website at www.ianallanpublishing.com

Distributed in the United States of America and Canada by BookMasters Distribution Services.

Copyright
Illegal copying and selling of publications deprives authors, publishers and booksellers of income, without which there would be no investment in new publications. Unauthorised versions of publications are also likely to be inferior in quality and contain incorrect information. You can help by reporting copyright infringements and acts of piracy to the Publisher or the UK Copyright Service.

Introduction

This album of previously unpublished colour photographs illustrates why during the demise of BR steam in the 1960s railway enthusiasts flocked to the South of England. The route to Bournemouth was the final steam-worked main line out of London, the Brockenhurst–Lymington Pier line was the last steam-operated passenger branch (Clapham Junction–Kensington Olympia is not a branch!), the Isle of Wight provided travel in pre-Grouping carriages hauled by Victorian locomotives, and the Havant–Hayling Island branch was worked by the oldest locomotives in the country, these being around 90 years old.

I was fortunate to be able to experience some of these workings, making a couple of pilgrimages to the Isle of Wight before steam was eradicated and visiting the Hayling Island branch as a 14-year-old in 1961. In those days I would often ask the driver if I could come into the cab and was used to climbing up onto the footplate. I was amazed to find, at Havant station, that, far from ascending, I seemed to be descending into the cab of the locomotive, so diminutive were the Class A1X 'Terriers'! It was also ironic that, three years after the Bluebell Railway commenced operations using its preserved 'Terrier' (*Stepney*), one could still ride behind an example in normal service!

Steam on the Southern lasted until July 1967, but most of the pictures selected for this book are earlier than this, recalling times when locomotives were usually kept in a presentable state. Indeed, some images go back to 1949 and depict locomotives in pre-nationalisation livery. Surprisingly, one of the rarest photographs is probably of what at first sight appears to be a commonplace 'O2' tank, until the number is checked out and the locomotive revealed to have been withdrawn in 1955 — making this possibly the only colour image of the locomotive in question.

The Solent is the stretch of water between the Isle of Wight and the mainland west of Southampton (Spithead is the strait to the east), but restricting the book to the Solent area would probably have meant covering only the Lymington branch and the Isle of Wight. To broaden interest, coverage has been extended westwards to Bournemouth West, bringing in Somerset & Dorset ('S&D') services, east to Portsmouth and Hayling Island and north to include the New Forest, Southampton and Eastleigh.

A few of the photographs are mine, but I have relied heavily on the work of other enthusiasts, and my grateful thanks go to Arthur and Neil Davenport, Michael Allen, Vernon Murphy, Nick Lera, Bruce Jenkins, Ken Wightman, David Clark and Jim Oatway. Photographs by Marcus Eavis and Frank Hunt are reproduced courtesy of the Online Transport Archive and the Light Rail Transit Association (London Branch) respectively.

Finally, it should be noted that not all the scenes and subjects depicted in this book have vanished for ever. One fifth of the 'Terrier' fleet survives, despite some examples' having been broken up at the start of the last century. Two 'Terriers' formerly used on the Isle of Wight, together with the last Island 'O2' locomotive, provide the Isle of Wight Steam Railway with authentic motive power, hauling pre-Grouping coaches over a section of the Cowes–Newport line. There are even vintage electric trains operating in the area on the national network — ex-London Transport (LT) 1938 Tube stock between Ryde and Shanklin and British Railways (BR) slam-door Mk 1 units on the Lymington branch. There remains much to interest railway enthusiasts visiting the Solent area.

Kevin R. McCormack
Ashtead, Surrey
December 2009

Left: The section of the Ryde–Ventnor line beyond its present terminus at Shanklin closed on 18 April 1966 amid controversy, for in the summer months Ventnor attracted large numbers of passengers. In this view Class O2 No 22 *Brading* stands ready to leave Ventnor for Ryde, entailing its burrowing through St Boniface Down, behind. *Frank Hunt / LRTA collection*

Above: The Gosport branch opened in 1841, but its importance soon diminished once the direct line to neighbouring Portsmouth was opened. Passenger services were withdrawn in 1953, and goods services in 1969. The branch ran from Fareham to both Lee-on-the-Solent and to Gosport (the line split at Fort Brockenhurst) and on 3 October 1965 was visited by a railtour hauled by Bulleid Class Q1 No 33020 (with No 33027 at the rear). *Vernon Murphy*

Left: Until May 1964 the branch from Brockenhurst to Lymington had been for many years associated with the LSWR 'M7' class. In this view dating from 21 July 1962 No 30029 shunts boat-train stock at the terminus, Lymington Pier, which was the mainland connection for ferries to Yarmouth, on the Isle of Wight. *Bruce Jenkins*

Above: Boat trains were a feature of the branch during summer months, and on 11 August 1962 one such train from Lymington Pier is seen leaving Brockenhurst behind ex-South Eastern & Chatham Railway (SECR) Class N 2-6-0 No 31816, built in 1922. *Bruce Jenkins*

Above: The 'Pines Express' from Manchester to Bournemouth was the S&D's most prestigious train, but, as a precursor to the line's closure, the service was diverted via Oxford, Reading, Basingstoke and Southampton after 8 September 1962. On its new routeing, the train is seen near Sway, southwest of Brockenhurst, hauled by unrebuilt Bulleid Pacific No 34103 *Calstock. Vernon Murphy*

Right: Ships arriving at Southampton did not only bring passengers. Goods and parcels trains were also a feature of operations in this area. Early in 1967 rebuilt Bulleid Pacific No 34104 *Bere Alston* approaches Millbrook, the first station west of Southampton. Freight traffic here has greatly increased since the Freightliner terminal was built behind the station. *Vernon Murphy*

Above and right: No 31 *Chale* and No 28 *Ashey* at Ashey! The old
station building, here lying derelict in September 1965 after
being replaced by a halt on the opposite side of the line, has now
been converted into a private residence and has the pleasure of
the Isle of Wight Steam Railway's restored Class O2 No 24
Calbourne passing by instead of these scruffy examples.
Author (both)

Eastleigh Works, where engines were hatched, patched and despatched! The LSWR moved its railway works from Nine Elms in London, where space was limited, to Eastleigh in 1909, having created a carriage and wagon works there in 1891. Ironically there is a dearth of genuine Southern locomotives in this view of the repair shops: in the foreground is an unidentified Standard Class 4 2-6-0, while in the background stand Nos 75077 and 41305, as well as an LT ex-Great Western Railway (GWR) pannier tank. *Ken Wightman*

Close to Eastleigh Works was the running shed, and in this view
a former LBSCR locomotive has arrived in the form of Class K
2-6-0 No 32344. The locomotive is buffered up to Class B4 0-4-0
dock tank No 30096, better known today as *Normandy* on the
Bluebell Railway. *Ken Wightman*

Left and above: Bournemouth West on 1 April 1949 finds Class LN (Lord Nelson) No 30862 *Lord Collingwood* still sporting Southern Railway malachite green with black and yellow lining, albeit displaying its BR identity, while one-time Somerset & Dorset Railway No 57, an 0-6-0 built by Armstrong, Whitworth & Co in 1922, remains in its subsequent LMS guise as it works an S&D local train. *Neil Davenport (both)*

Left: Class O2 No 33 *Bembridge* crosses the River Medina as it approaches Newport on a Cowes–Ryde train in the summer of 1960. Pre-Grouping rolling stock was used not out of sentimentality or for economic reasons but because more modern carriages were too high and too long to operate on the island. The loading-gauge was almost a foot lower than on the mainland, and there were several sharp curves and structures close to the track. On electrification, height considerations dictated the use of ex-LT Tube stock rather than surface stock. *Marcus Eavis / Online Transport Archive*

Above: Immaculately presented Class O2 No 32 *Bonchurch* prepares to leave Cowes with a train to Newport and Ryde in the summer of 1960. The line from Smallbrook (junction with the Ventnor line) to Cowes closed on 21 February 1966, but part of it lives again: starting in 1971, a five-mile section between Smallbrook Junction and Wootton has been reopened in stages by the Isle of Wight Steam Railway. *Marcus Eavis / Online Transport Archive*

Left: Lots of ladies' hats head for the Cunard liner *Queen Elizabeth* (the original one, destined to meet a fiery end in Hong Kong harbour) as 'USA' tank No DS233, formerly No 30061 and normally based at Redbridge sleeper depot, shunts at Southampton Docks on 9 June 1964. The Southern bought 14 of these American-built engines for service and one for spare parts, all constructed by Vulcan Ironworks apart from this example and the spare-parts locomotive, which were produced by H. K. Porter. *Author's collection*

Above: Replacements for the ageing Class M7 tanks on the Lymington branch came in the form of Standard Class 4 tanks and the smaller LMS-designed Ivatt Class 2s. No 41264 of the latter type stands at the small engine shed beside Lymington Town station on 6 November 1966. *David Clark*

Above: The structure that symbolised the Hayling Island branch was the wooden Langstone Harbour railway bridge, over which no locomotive heavier than a 'Terrier' was permitted (and only examples fitted with spark-arresting chimneys, to reduce the risk of the bridge catching fire!). In this view the train has just passed over the opening section of the bridge and is heading for North Hayling behind No 32678, one of three 'Terriers' rescued by Butlins, this one being preserved on the Kent & East Sussex Railway. *Ken Wightman*

Right: The 10 preserved 'Terriers' had some unlikely saviours — the aforementioned holiday-camp operator, a brewery, a Canadian museum and, in the case of No 32650, also seen on the Hayling Island branch, a local council. Originally named *Whitechapel*, this locomotive was bought by the Borough of Sutton & Cheam (now the London Borough of Sutton) for display in the new town centre, but this never materialised, and in September 1964 it steamed to the Kent & East Sussex Railway, where it remained on loan until its recent transfer to the Spa Valley Railway at Tunbridge Wells. *Ken Wightman*

Class N15 'King Arthur' No 30781 *Sir Aglovale* simmers at
Eastleigh shed on 2 March 1960. Completed in July 1925, the
locomotive became one of the last survivors despite its appalling
external condition here, not being withdrawn until May 1962.
Jim Oatway

Contrasting with the newly overhauled locomotive which it is pushing on 10 August 1961, this grimy Eastleigh Works shunter, 64-year-old '700'-class 0-6-0 No 30306, has only another eight months to go before withdrawal. Built by Dübs & Co of Glasgow, these Drummond-designed locomotives had resembled the Caledonian Railway's 'Standard Goods' ('Jumbos') until they were superheated (from 1919), receiving a front-end extension in the process. *Jim Oatway*

'Lord Nelson' No 30854 *Howard of Effingham* approaches Southampton Central with an up Bournemouth express in the summer of 1957. The locomotive is running with a bogie tender, enabling the carrying of extra coal and water for long-distance running on the South Western main line, there being no water troughs on the Southern. The entire class of 16 locomotives was withdrawn between August 1961 and October 1962, replaced by Bulleid Pacifics whose reliability had improved following rebuilding. *Ken Wightman*

Unrebuilt Bulleid Pacific No 34055 *Fighter Pilot* stands on the turntable at Bournemouth shed on 22 April 1962. No fewer than 110 of these 'West Country'/'Battle of Britain' Light Pacifics were built, between 1945 and 1950, and this one was among the first three to be withdrawn, in June 1963. *Jim Oatway*

Ringwood station, where Standard Class 4 No 75074 is seen in June 1967, was on a cross-country line (avoiding Bournemouth) which ran from Lymington Junction (outside Brockenhurst) to Broadstone Junction, where it joined up with the S&D, to the west of Bournemouth. When opened in 1847 to link Southampton and Dorchester this route served places with sizeable populations, but its importance declined as Bournemouth expanded. Ringwood station closed to passengers on 4 May 1964 and to freight on 7 August 1967. *Nick Lera*

Adams Class O2 No 33 *Bembridge* heads towards Smallbrook Junction with a Ventnor train in September 1965. The stock is composed of ex-LSWR and ex-LBSCR carriages (the latter having flatter roofs) with most of their wooden side panelling intact and only limited replacement with sheet metal. *Author*

Left and above: The ungated level crossing at Canute Road, between Southampton Terminus station and the Eastern Docks, was controlled manually using a red flag and a bell. Pictured at this location on 16 June 1967 and 10 March 1963 respectively are unrebuilt 'West Country' Pacific No 34023 *Blackmore Vale* (now preserved on the Bluebell Railway), and preserved Class T9 No 120, formerly No 30120. The road name commemorates King Canute the Great, the Viking who ruled England from 1016 until 1035 and is reputed to have got his feet wet at Southampton when he failed to stop the tide. *Marcus Eavis / Online Transport Archive; David Clark*

In 1933/4 four Stroudley 'E1' 0-6-0 tanks were sent to the Isle of Wight to haul heavy goods trains, but as freight traffic diminished in the 1950s they became redundant, and they were withdrawn between 1956 and 1960. Occasionally they were used on passenger trains, as demonstrated here at Newport on 1 September 1955 by No 4 *Wroxall*, dating from 1878. *Neil Davenport*

Pram alert at Brading during steam's final summer (1966) on the Isle of Wight as No 20 *Shanklin* waits to take the 4.55pm from Shanklin to Ryde. Until the branch was closed in 1953 trains from Bembridge would have entered Brading from this direction and used the down island platform. *Marcus Eavis / Online Transport Archive*

After skirting the sea 'U'-class 2-6-0 No 31804 (formerly 'River'-class 2-6-4 tank No A804 *River Tamar*, rebuilt as a tender engine in 1928) approaches Mount Pleasant Crossing, Southampton. The date is 2 September 1962, and the service is the 2.15pm from Portsmouth & Southsea to Cardiff. The recently constructed Northam train depot is now situated nearby. *Michael Allen*

Cars are boarding the Isle of Wight ferry to Yarmouth on 7 July 1962 as Class M7 No 30029 prepares to leave Lymington Pier with the Brockenhurst push-and-pull train. Opened in 1858, the branch originally ran only as far as Lymington Town but was extended to the pier in 1884 after the independent company which built and operated the line was taken over by the LSWR (in 1878). *Nick Lera*

Above: A brand-new and seemingly unnamed 'Merchant Navy' (which doesn't appear to belong to anyone!) prepares to depart from Bournemouth Central on 19 April 1949. Resplendent in SR malachite green with yellow lining, No 35030 *Elder Dempster Lines* has its nameplates covered up pending the official naming ceremony. *Neil Davenport*

Right: Bombed in 1941, when no fewer than 20 locomotives were damaged, Fratton engine shed remained operational until November 1959, after which it was used for storing locomotives, including some earmarked for possible preservation. Sadly, fortune did not look kindly on Class L1 No 31757, seen here in the roundhouse on 1 April 1962, with the result that there are no Maunsell rebuilds of Wainwright 4-4-0s (Classes D1, E1 and L1) in existence today. *Jim Oatway*

Above: The 10.50am from Bristol Temple Meads to Portsmouth Harbour enters Portsmouth & Southsea High Level on 3 August 1963 behind Standard Class 5 No 73065; the low-level terminus can be seen on the left. The station was opened in 1847, but the only passenger service was to Brighton. Not until 1859 would through trains run to London, and in the interim Portsmuthians had either to travel to London via Brighton or to take the ferry to Gosport. *Michael Allen*

Right: With a warning 'NEXT STATION FOR BOATS' sign secured to the station nameboard, Class M7 No 30052 arrives at Lymington Town on 3 June 1963, propelling the 5pm from Brockenhurst to Lymingon Pier. Within a year the late-Victorian 'M7s' would be replaced by locomotives more than 50 years younger. *Michael Allen*

Left: 'Lord Nelson' No 30851 *Sir Francis Drake* reposes at Eastleigh shed on 2 June 1959. These powerful locomotives, designed by Maunsell and built between 1926 and 1929, were intended for heavy express-passenger work but did not reach their full potential until blastpipe and chimney modifications were carried out by Bulleid in 1938. Their introduction had resulted in the downgrading of the 'N15s' ('King Arthurs') to lighter passenger trains, although these locomotives, along with the 'Lord Nelsons', would last until 1962. *Jim Oatway*

Above: After the earlier Urie 'N15s' had all been withdrawn (by March 1958) it was the turn of the later Maunsell examples, No 30766 *Sir Geriant* being the second to succumb. Withdrawn in December 1958, it is seen here at Eastleigh in the process of being broken up. *Jim Oatway*

Above: Open landscape and ponies typify the New Forest, traversed by the Southampton–Bournemouth line. A Standard Class 4 2-6-4 tank hauls a local train between Beaulieu Road and Brockenhurst. *Vernon Murphy*

Right: The station before Beaulieu Road is Lyndhurst Road, nowadays known as Ashurst (New Forest). Seen passing on 10 June 1965 is Giesl-ejector-fitted Bulleid Light Pacific No 34064 *Fighter Command*, the 1,000th locomotive built at Brighton Works. *David Clark*

41

Left: Southampton Docks in the late 1950s, starring an MG TF sports car, with a supporting cast of three ex-LBSCR locomotives — Billinton Class E2 0-6-0 No 32109 (the last of a batch of five built with extended tanks) and Stroudley 'E1s' Nos 32689 and 32151. *Ken Wightman*

Above: The chunky 'USA' tanks which the SR had purchased in 1946/7, primarily to replace the elderly ex-LSWR 'B4' dock shunters, were themselves superseded by diesels, as apparent from this picture taken on 1 September 1962 at the Docks engine shed. *David Clark*

Above and right: With the reinstatement of the all-over roof, Bournemouth Central station (nowadays simply 'Bournemouth') currently looks much better than it did on 6 September 1966 when Standard Class 5 No 73065 was departing with the 11.07am Bournemouth–Waterloo, followed shortly after by rebuilt 'West Country' No 34013 *Okehampton* with the 11.25am Weymouth–Waterloo. This latter locomotive was one of 60 Light Pacifics (from a total of 110) rebuilt between 1957 and 1961, before the programme was abandoned in the light of the Modernisation Plan designed to eradicate steam traction as quickly as possible. *Marcus Eavis / Online Transport Archive (both)*

Drummond's T9 4-4-0s, introduced in 1899, were coming to the end of their illustrious careers when No 30729 was photographed at Eastleigh on 2 June 1959, having just dropped its fire. However, this locomotive was to live on a little longer; three months later the photographer found it working at Wadebridge, in Cornwall. *Jim Oatway*

The Bulleid Light Pacifics, like the heavier 'Merchant Navys', were designed during World War 2, when the emphasis was on cost savings and ease of maintenance. The locomotives had several novel features including wheels with holes (to decrease weight and eliminate the risk of broken spokes), chain-driven valve gear in a sealed oil bath (to reduce the need for lubrication) and 'air-smoothed' casing (to facilitate cleaning, e.g. through use of carriage-washing plants). Seen passing through Bitterne station, on the route from Southampton to Fareham, with the 11.10am Plymouth–Brighton on 2 September 1962 is 'Battle of Britain' No 34067 *Tangmere*, a locomotive destined to be saved from Dai Woodham's legendary scrapyard (and currently giving great pleasure working steam specials on the main line), while pictured on 3 October 1966, having just brought a railtour into Portsmouth Harbour station, built on a wooden pier extending into the harbour, is 'West Country' No 34002 *Salisbury*. *Michael Allen; Vernon Murphy*

Above: As evidenced by this view from a passing train in July 1964, Ryde Works repaired locomotives, carriages and wagons in somewhat spartan conditions. Seen receiving attention under the hoist is Class O2 No 31 *Chale*, built in 1890 as LSWR No 180 and transferred to the island in 1927. *Author*

Right: A proliferation of signage dominates this view of Sandown station in July 1964 as No 27 *Merstone* prepares to depart for Ventnor. Trains from Newport and Merstone had used the abandoned face of the up island platform until that line closed in 1956. Note the leaking Westinghouse brake pump, which has a shield around it to protect bystanders. *Author*

Above: There is no sign of declining patronage on the Hayling Island branch in the final summer of operation as Class A1X No 32650 (formerly *Whitechapel* and now *Sutton*) approaches Langstone Bridge with a full load on 28 July 1963. The goods van has probably been added to carry an overflow of passenger luggage. *David Clark*

Right: Meanwhile the real *Sutton*, No 32661 — which the Council narrowly failed to secure — hurries away from Havant on its way to Hayling Island. This was the last 'Terrier' to be scrapped, in September 1963 — 62 years after the first four met with a similar fate! *Ken Wightman*

Left and above: Pictures of Southampton Central station taken in the 1960s, prior to rebuilding and the destruction of the magnificent clock tower, tend to feature Bulleid Pacifics. By way of a change, here are two less-usual visitors on 2 September 1962, reflecting the importance of freight traffic handled by the docks — Standard Class 9F 2-10-0 No 92128 and ex-GWR '2884' 2-8-0 No 3802, the latter now preserved on the Llangollen Railway. *Michael Allen (both)*

Left: Adams Class T3 express passenger 4-4-0 No 563, the last survivor of its class and withdrawn as long ago as 1945, looks somewhat jaded at Eastleigh Works on 2 March 1960. Built by the LSWR at Nine Elms in 1893, this locomotive currently forms part of the National Railway Museum's 'Locomotion' exhibition at Shildon, Co Durham. *Jim Oatway*

Above: The last 'King Arthur' (Class N15) to remain in service, No 30770 *Sir Prianius*, makes a splendid sight at Eastleigh shed on 2 September 1962, two months before its withdrawal. Fortunately we can today enjoy the sight of classmate No 30777 *Sir Lamiel* hauling specials on the main line. *David Clark*

Left: Designed to work express freight trains, the Urie and Maunsell 'S15' 4-6-0s were versatile locomotives which were frequently used on passenger trains. In the summer of 1964 No 30840, from the later, Maunsell batch, passes a pair of former Pullman cars converted as camping coaches as it hauls an inter-regional train of Midland stock through Sway, the first station south-west of Brockenhurst. *Vernon Murphy*

Above: Returning to its old haunts after being displaced by 'USA' tanks at the end of World War 2, Adams Class B4 0-4-0 dock tank No 30096 (formerly *Normandy*) has brought a railtour to Southampton Ocean Terminal on 6 April 1963. Built in 1893, this locomotive was the last of its class to be overhauled (in March 1961) and following withdrawal in October 1963 was sold to a fuel merchant for further use at Southampton Docks before arriving on the Bluebell Railway in 1972. *Ken Wightman*

Following bridge-strengthening, larger, more modern locomotives capable of climbing the Mendip Hills unaided were introduced on the S&D, commencing in 1938 with some Stanier 'Black Fives'. One such locomotive, No 44826, enters Bournemouth West on 19 April 1949. *Neil Davenport*

'Battle of Britain' Pacific No 34061 *73 Squadron* is in the process of being coaled up at Bournemouth shed in this view recorded on 14 April 1949, two years after the locomotive entered service.
Arthur Davenport

Above and right: Taken within minutes of one another in September 1965, these two photographs illustrate the unusual concept of parallel single-line running, which outside the main summer-holiday season was a feature of Isle of Wight operations between Ryde St John's Road and Smallbrook Junction. Class O2 No 29 *Alverstone*, built in 1891, takes the track on the left to Newport and Cowes, while No 33 *Bembridge*, dating from 1892, heads for Shanklin and Ventnor. *Author (both)*

Above: The last Stroudley Class E1 to remain in service, No 32694, built in 1875 and withdrawn in 1961, stands at Southampton Docks on 17 July 1960. One class member survives, No B110 *Burgundy*, sold to a colliery in 1927 and now preserved on the East Somerset Railway. *Michael Allen*

Right: Devoid of its nameplates, rebuilt Bulleid 'Battle of Britain' No 34090 *Sir Eustace Missenden — Southern Railway* approaches St Denys on 27 May 1967 with a Bournemouth–Waterloo train composed of at least four Bulleid carriages. The locomotive was built at Brighton Works in 1949 and named after the SR's last General Manager, in recognition of the wartime efforts and sacrifices of its employees. *Author's collection*

Above: The Southern's last steam-hauled Pullman train, the 'Bournemouth Belle' from Waterloo, coasts through New Milton, between Sway and Hinton Admiral, behind rebuilt 'Merchant Navy' No 35023 *Holland-Afrika Line*. The 'Belle' used to run to Bournemouth West until this station closed to passengers in September 1965, after which it terminated at Bournemouth Central. *Vernon Murphy*

Right: Southampton Terminus was the original station serving both town and docks and was opened by the London & Southampton Railway in 1840. Closed to passengers in 1966, its fine Italianate-style main building is now used for commercial purposes. This 1958 view depicts Class S15 No 30511, from the original (Urie) batch dating from 1920/1. *Ken Wightman*

Probably Maunsell's most successful design was the Class V ('Schools') 4-4-0, of which 40 were constructed between 1930 and 1935. Built primarily for the Hastings line, with its narrow tunnels which had received additional internal lining after one collapsed, these locomotives were reputed to be the most powerful 4-4-0s in Europe. Bulleid modified more than half the class by fitting a multiple blastpipe and wide chimney, but No 30902 *Wellington*, pictured at Eastleigh shed on 28 March 1962, remained unaltered. *Jim Oatway*

Represented by No 30133 on 15 March 1961 at Eastleigh station is another highly successful locomotive type, Drummond's 'M7' 0-4-4T, of which 105 were built between 1897 and 1911. Testament to their competence is the fact that, apart from one which was unsuccessfully rebuilt and another which fell down the lift shaft allowing access to the subterranean Waterloo & City line, the class remained intact until 1957, and in virtually original condition. Most worked initially on London suburban services, from which they were displaced by electrification. *Jim Oatway*

Above and right: The Totton–Fawley branch came late on the scene, the catalyst being the construction in 1920/1 of the oil terminal at Fawley (which is the reason the line remains open today for freight). However, passenger services, which commenced in 1925, were never well patronised and were withdrawn from 14 February 1966. In our first view, recorded on 20 March 1966, two 'USA' tanks, Nos 30073 and 30064, head a railtour through Marchwood, one of two intermediate stations (the other being Hythe), while in the second, dating from 9 April 1967, Nos 30069 (still in old livery) and 30064 bring a special into Fawley. *Vernon Murphy (both)*

The author was not to know when he took this picture of No 24 *Calbourne* leaving Smallbrook Junction for Ashey in September 1965 that, thanks to the Isle of Wight Steam Railway, No 24 would still be running along this stretch of line in the 21st century! However, it is extraordinary that a fleet of Victorian, ex-mainland locomotives, still extant as late as 1967, should attract no other buyers. *Author*

Bulleid 'West Country' Pacific No 34002 *Salisbury* hurries along near Christchurch in the summer of 1966. In their unrebuilt form these locomotives could certainly move, but, as was the case with the 'Merchant Navy' class, leakage from the oil bath that encased the valve gear could cause adhesion problems and, in extreme cases, ignite accumulations of oil and grease on the boiler lagging. *Vernon Murphy*

Left and above: Sir Billy Butlin, the holiday-camp operator, saved eight steam locomotives from being scrapped, three of which — *Duchess of Hamilton*, *Royal Scot* and the less-prestigious one depicted here — had all represented Britain overseas. Class A1X No 32640, seen working a Havant–Hayling Island service on 17 June 1962 at Langston station and approaching Langstone Bridge, was a Gold Medal winner at the Paris Exhibition of 1878 and, having from 1902 to 1947 been based on the Isle of Wight, has now returned to the island as No 11 *Newport*. The former LBSCR station nameboard, using an early spelling of the village, survived to the end. *Nick Lera (both)*

Above: In July 1955, carrying a reporting number which was a feature of busy summer Saturdays on the Isle of Wight's railways, No 31 *Chale* has come off Ryde Pier and arrived at Ryde Esplanade before descending into Esplanade Tunnel to reach Ryde St John's Road. *Bruce Jenkins*

Right: Whereas No 31 was to survive until 1967, No 15 *Cowes*, seen here at Newport on 19 September 1955, would be withdrawn a few weeks after this picture was taken. *Neil Davenport*

Left: On 20 March 1966 No 31639, the final member of the 50-strong Maunsell 'U' class, waits to take over a railtour at Fareham station. The 'U' was a larger-wheeled version of the 'N', the first 20 being rebuilds of 'River' 2-6-4 tanks, the remaining 30 entirely new locomotives. Four survive, including No 31806, the former *River Torridge*. *Major Cotton / author's collection*

Above: No 30852 *Sir Walter Raleigh*, built in 1928 as the third member of the 'Lord Nelson' class, pulls out of Southampton Central station with a down Bournemouth train. These locomotives were named after famous admirals in an attempt to create an association, in the public's mind, with maritime activities and thereby promote the SR's services to and from the Channel ports. *Ken Wightman*

Above and right: The closure of the Hayling Island branch, on
3 November 1963, was marked by the running on that day of a
railtour from Waterloo. These photographs show the special
approaching Fareham behind ex-LSWR Urie Class S15 No 30512
and at North Hayling behind ex-LBSCR Class A1X No 32636
(formerly *Fenchurch*). The latter had been the first 'Terrier'
to enter service (on 9 September 1872) and the first to be
withdrawn by the LBSCR (in 1898, when it was sold) and,
having been acquired by the SR in 1926, was by now the oldest
locomotive in BR service. Withdrawn immediately after the
railtour, it arrived at its new home, the Bluebell Railway, on
13 May 1964 and has since been restored cosmetically to its
original Class A1 condition. *Ken Wightman; author's collection*

The naming of the 'Merchant Navy' class after shipping companies using Southampton Docks was a more blatant attempt by the SR to emphasise its maritime credentials. In this view from the summer of 1964 No 35011

General Steam Navigation hurries a train of Bulleid coaching stock through Pokesdown station, between Christchurch and Bournemouth Central. *Vernon Murphy*

18/7